TO SAVE THE FALLING NATIONS

A Physical Task for Spiritual Leaders

Tunji Oreyingbo, PH.D.

WESTBOW
PRESS®
A DIVISION OF THOMAS NELSON
& ZONDERVAN

Scripture taken from the New King James Version®. Copyright © 1982 by Thomas Nelson. Used by permission. All rights reserved.

WestBow Press books may be ordered through booksellers or by contacting:

WestBow Press
A Division of Thomas Nelson & Zondervan
1663 Liberty Drive
Bloomington, IN 47403
www.westbowpress.com
1 (866) 928-1240

Cover Layout designed by: Tunji Ishola.
Cover Image by: Freepik.com

ISBN: 978-1-5127-7043-8 (sc)
ISBN: 978-1-5127-7044-5 (e)

Library of Congress Control Number: 2016921303

Print information available on the last page.

WestBow Press rev. date: 01/27/2017

CONTENTS

DEDICATION

To my parents:

Chief Samuel and Sola Oreyingbo
Who introduced me to Christ and instilled
in me a genuine love for others.

FIRST WORDS

I believe in the call of God upon the lives of the Spiritual leaders of our time. I believe that each Christian leader has the ability to positively equip mankind and do things that will get the world to a greater height. It is also my believe that the Christian ministry leaders in the third world nations have more roles to play in helping these falling nations than they currently play.

This book, therefore, is a call on spiritual leaders, especially Christian leaders, to take up the task of presenting themselves and the Church as the lights of the world by speaking truth to themselves, to political leaders, to their followers, and to the general populace. This is a task with the potential to save nations from ruin and restore their lost glories.

Though this book bears only my name on its cover as the author, it is the product of many minds. I want to thank Sanctified Word Ministry leadership for the opportunity to present parts of this material which emanated from numerous teachings. This gives ample opportunity to advance on the journey of living the Book – The Bible. Perhaps all books need be lived while they are written and beyond. A statement that is undoubtedly true of books like this.

I wish to express my appreciation to my wife Rachel, and children: Esther, Oreoluwa, and Lydia for their patience and tolerance during the research for and the writing of this work.

I wish to thank Pastor Femi Olawale and Pastor Alan Smith for all their helpful guidance which helped in fine tuning this book. I owe special thanks to Dr. Stephen O. Solanke for reading the manuscript and offering his valuable comments. I thank my friend Dickson E. Arughu for motivating me to higher achievements. I thank Deacon Segun Odunuga, Sade Odunuga, Dr. Wale Oreyingbo, Foluso Oreyingbo, Dr. Dayo Ogundare, Deacon Ndubisi Oyindo, Dapo Ige, Bisi Ige, Remi Adeyale, Jaderson Adeyale, Ajibike Bayo-Oreyingbo, Bayo Oreyingbo, and Omolara Arughu for their feedbacks and for appreciating my seminars.

It is with deep gratitude that I express my appreciation to the following people who have been helpful to me in my Christian journey: Bishop Seth I. Kale, Pastor Tayo Ojajuni, Victor Omoruyi Ogunsuyi, Pastor Folarin Akinsola, Demion Platt, Pastor Kunle Fafiolu, and Deacon Tunji Ishola.

Above all, I thank God for his enabling presence. To him belong all glory, praise, and honour! The English translation of the Bible used throughout is the New King James version, unless otherwise noted.

May this book inspire and encourage Christian leaders to take their callings seriously and perpetually do all that is needed to bring out the best from their followers.

CHAPTER ONE

INTRODUCTION

He was in prison. Not that he had been tried and sentenced, but he was still awaiting trial. He probably had been under this condition for more than a year. Guarded by soldiers, chained on both legs with a rough iron that weighed around seven kilograms, he was confined to a dungeon where he barely saw the light of day. Despite his dilapidating condition, he still hoped for a favorable verdict and his ultimate release. He was incarcerated not because he was a criminal, but for his conviction. A conviction so strong that he could not keep it to himself, rather, he gladly shared it with those he came in contact with. To limit the spread of his message, he had been held captive by the governing authority of his time. He, however, could not help but stay in touch with those who heard his testimony prior to his imprisonment, and had believed his message. Thus, while in Rome as a prisoner, he wrote numerous letters. Here is an excerpt from one of his letters:

> I hope to send Timothy to you soon…I have no one else like Timothy, who genuinely cares about your welfare. All the others care only for themselves and not for what matters to Jesus Christ. Philippians 2:20–21 (NLT)

Is this not the condition of Africa today? A continent that has nations filled with millions of apostles, prophets, pastors, reverends, bishops, evangelists, deacons, deaconesses and a host of others with numerous hierarchical titles from the Church, yet it is sinking. The land is dying under the filthy hands of corruption with only a handful of God's protagonists acting as voices in the wilderness. Many of our so-called men and women of God are merely after earthly treasures. Very few are like Paul or even Timothy in their Christ-centered loyalty to the Gospel, and commitment to the welfare of the flock.

Africa remains the poorest continent on earth though it is the second most-populous continent. It had an estimated population of 1.033 billion people in 2013, of which about 50 percent are Christians. In the 2013 report of Transparency International, around 80 percent of African people live on less than two US dollars a day. Poverty is killing Africa. These poor people have very low access to information, and they remain uneducated. They are not enlightened, and many do not know their rights. Their lack of exposure leaves them more vulnerable to be exploited, and this is one area in which the Church is most needed.

The Sting of Corruption

Africa is in a hopeless situation. Corruption in the continent is endemic and has made the continent the poorest in the world. Poverty is on the increase in every nook and cranny of the continent.

In Africa, our petty thieves are maimed and killed while the highly placed ones are usually celebrated and eventually elected or appointed into public offices. Nearly all African countries are bedeviled with decayed and decaying infrastructure. Our hospitals have become mortuaries, with children dying in the thousands daily. Our airlines, railways, shipping lines, and public road transportation system have collapsed and are majorly abandoned. There is no portable water in our towns and cities, not to talk of the rural areas. Our main source of power is diesel-powered, privately owned electricity generators. The nations are continually choked with rising international debts. Our schools have become rubbles and tutors are unpaid for several months. Cultism is on the rise in our high schools and post-secondary institutions. People are terrorized by armed robbers in their homes and on the roads. The economy is in shambles with exchange rates of African currencies to internationally accepted currencies plummeting drastically over the years. Ritual killing is the order of the day. Militant insurgency is getting strengthened while the nations` military are continually disarmed. Terrorism is claiming thousands of lives annually. The leaders in our Churches are becoming fatter at the expense of their vulnerable followers. Our courts are conscience dead and cannot uphold the rights of the citizens. Our police stations have turned to dens of robbers. Our refineries are grounded. Kidnapping is at its peak. Our narrow-minded young men have turned to fraud and armed robbery, while our susceptible young women are engaged in prostitution. Baby factories and human trafficking are now at great heights, while trade in human body parts is prevalent. The vast majority of the people are pauperized and life expectancy in Africa has dropped drastically.

Every sector of the continent is plagued by corruption, with the Churches not exempted. Our saints are being sidetracked, ridiculed and demonized, while the thieves in public offices are much-admired and canonized. The continent's situation brings to light the word of Isaiah. He says: "Your princes are rebellious, and companions of thieves; everyone loves bribes and follows after rewards. They do not defend the fatherless, nor does the cause of the widow come before them" (Isaiah 1:23). In the midst of this pathetic situation, some writings are sanguine and profess with hope that Africa's tomorrow will be alright while others portray discouragement that corruption is here to stay and no one can do anything about it. Some again opine that corruption is an essential part of growth – and every developed nation experienced it along the way.

However one views it, corruption in Africa is killing the continent. The love of money has boosted the upward movement of evil in the African nations and the continent is falling. Ethics is lacking in all institutions of the continent. Corruption is an epidemic in Africa, and the continent is gradually becoming a tragic icon. What can we do? How can we fight and conquer corruption that is killing us more than any other disease?

Ngozi Okonjo-Iweala, while talking about how the economic team which worked on the reforms of Nigeria did its work in her book – *Reforming the Unreformable,* posits:

> That fighting corruption successfully would require four crucial and inseparable ingredients. The first was political will and commitment from very top. The second was specificity in terms of identifying the most damaging forms of corruption and focusing on these. The third was developing measurable indicators of success or other means of demonstrating success. We strongly believe that the more the Nigerian public could see a serious, successful fight against corruption, the more they would own the fight and demand that it continue. Finally, we needed the ability to withstand personal intimidation or threats, and to forge on with the fight.[1]

Though Okonjo-Iweala's book is written specifically to address the Nigerian situation, the issue at stake is continental and affects all African nations. The ingredients too are universally viable to all the nations. In this light, I would add that a renewing of the minds of those at the top as well as those at the bottom against corruption and its every element is crucial to our reformation as a people,

---

[1] Okonjo-Iweala, Ngozi. *Reforming the Unreformable. Lessons from Nigeria.* Cambridge, Massachusetts: The MIT Press, 2012, 87.

and needs to be put in place. This is where the spiritual leaders come into the picture. Our Churches need to take up their task as institutions that disapprove of injustice and be champions of truth in all its facets.

Championing this course by the Church requires the commitment of our spiritual leaders since belief grows gradually by hearing and hearing the word of reformation. It is obvious from past experiences that having the military take over the executive arm of government has not been helpful in the long run. Elected civilians have proven no better too. No system of government seems to work in any of the nations. It is not that these systems of government are ineffective, but greed and selfishness of the leaders that have filtered down to the followers have corrupted the systems. Our minds have become morally polluted and ethically impure. Corruption has eaten deep into the cores of an average person. There is wide disconnect between the doctrine and practice of the Church and how they applied to the wider community. Christian leaders now lend themselves to manipulations, to the profits of the 'powers that be' or acclaimed spiritually superior individuals and groups. It thus becomes a necessity for the Churches to wake up from their slumber and uphold the morality of faithfulness. For the Churches to be valuable in this regard, they first need to remove the planks from their own eyes. It is after this that they can see clearly and be able to remove the specks from the eyes of those within and without. Church leaders, therefore, must be ready to learn and make use of some key things as practiced by Apostle Paul.

Paul's Comport Principles

The Apostle Paul never projected himself in such a way as to be remembered as a model pedagogue, though it is not out of place to picture him as such. Certainly, the apostle wanted his converts and mentees to follow his examples and pass on what they saw in him to others after them. Many times in the Scripture he admonishes us to follow his example. Successful Church leadership is more than merely teaching the truth of God or giving instructions that relate to the Scripture. An apostle, pastor, reverend, evangelist or teacher of the word must go further. Pious words do not necessarily produce an effective disciple, but a holy life, which demonstrates godly attributes through clear thinking, speeches, and reputable conduct will do. Unquestionable characters always add vital pearl to the rank of any leader as well as influence the lives of the congregation. In fact the most important factor with which to rank any teacher is who he really is. One practical demonstration of integrity is worth more than scores of sermons. Apostle Paul believed and lived what he preached. Some of the ministerial principles he lived by are relevant, and are as useful to us today as they were to the first-century Church. Some of these principles are: Financial Transparency, Speaking Truth to the Authority, Financial Independence, and Teaching through Practice.

CHAPTER TWO

FINANCIAL TRANSPARENCY

But thanks be to God who puts the same earnest care for you into the heart of Titus. For he not only accepted the exhortation, but being more diligent, he went to you of his own accord. And we have sent with him the brother whose praise is in the gospel throughout all the Churches, and not only that, but who was also chosen by the Churches to travel with us with this gift, which is administered by us to the glory of the Lord Himself and to show your ready mind, avoiding this: that anyone should blame us in this lavish gift which is administered by us – providing honorable things, not only in the sight of the Lord, but also in the sight of men.

2 Corinthians 8:16–21

Transparency simply means the condition of being open. It is having intentions that are obvious to all that are concerned. It means to be plain and frank. It means to be unambiguous, straightforward, and crystal clear. It is the act of being without craftiness, disguise or concealment. It is allowing all parties involved in any situation to see the truth without an attempt to conceal or alter the facts. Transparency is not a passive act which aids distrust or suspicion; it is about active as well as pro-active disclosures which help in preventing personal agendas from thwarting a group's plan. Transparency encompasses sincerity, full disclosure, integrity, candidness, legal compliance, and many other features that allow people to deal reasonably and truthfully with one another.

2 Corinthians 8:16–21 explains how the monetary gathering from the Churches in the province of Achaia (which included Corinth) was to be delivered to the poor Christians in Jerusalem. This passage, in conjunction with the leading passage on the same subject (1 Corinthians 16:1–4) demonstrates how Paul established some basic paradigm which when followed resulted in healthy monetary gathering and disbursement within the Church.

Collection Strategy

One, Paul ensured that the gathering for the Jerusalem poor was made voluntary as a free will contribution and was completely optional. No specific amount or percentage of the donors' income was required for the collection. Each person was simply asked to give "according to how one proposes in his heart" (2 Corinthians 9:7). Paul, however, re-emphasized the planter's principle: "He who sows sparingly will also reap sparingly and he who sows bountifully will also reap bountifully" (2 Corinthians 9:6). A cleverly constructed preparatory statement aimed at strengthening the willpower of the donors.

Two, he ensured that the collection process was made convenient and comfortable to the donors – a weekly event. They were to be done on the first day of the week. "On the first day of the week let each one of you lay something aside, storing up as he may prosper" (1 Corinthians 16:2). The first day of the week is the day that Christians meet together for weekly service during the first-century AD (Acts 20:7). This was a directive which could have been aimed at eliminating any issue that may likely have occurred if each donor was to take their donation to the collection point at different times. It could be a way of encouraging all to be on attendance at the appointed days. It could also have been a move to make each and all donations obvious to more than the collector alone (Mathew 18:16; 2 Corinthians 13:1). In other words, any dispute between the donor and the collector as regards giving and collecting was eliminated through this process since the giving would not only have been witnessed by the giver and the collector but also by those present during the weekly fellowship.

Three, he ensured that all gatherings were to be made during his absence. "That there be no collection when I come" was his instruction (1 Corinthians 16:2b). This could have been to eliminate the need for him to know who had given more or who contributed less. Thus, he eliminated the human factor of favoring or preferring some of his congregants to others, based on their financial contributions. This could also be a strategy put in place by Paul to prevent the congregants from being pressurized to give more by his presence. Better still, it could be a way to ensure that the collection was fully done and accounts balanced prior to his visit. The only outstanding item at his arrival would then be: How to deliver the bounty to the Jerusalem Church.

Disbursement Strategy

The disbursement strategy was such that provided for openness, incorporating a procedure of checks and balances. Checks and balances can be defined as the various procedures set in place to reduce or eliminate mistakes as well as improper behavior. Paul ensured that the disbursement emissary was made up of a combination of people trusted and selected by Paul himself, and those trusted and appointed by the contributing Churches.

The number of people in the delivery team was not clearly stated. Paul's letter to the Church in Rome reveals that he went with the team to Jerusalem (Romans 15:25–26). Titus and "our brother whom we have often proved diligent in many things" (2 Corinthians 8:22) were both delegates appointed by Paul while the Churches of Achaia chose a prominent and unimpeachable brother "whose praise is in the gospel throughout all the Churches to travel with us with this gift" (2 Corinthians 8:18–19).

Reasons for Paul's Principle of Financial Transparency

Paul ensured that financial transparency was

demonstrated within his ministry. This was a principle which was not only demonstrated in the delivery of the money gathered, but was started right from the initial stage of collecting funds from the congregants. There seem to be four major reasons for Paul's principle of financial transparency.

Firstly, he wanted to nullify deceptive accusations from adulterating false teachers. These are teachers with whom Paul never wanted to be associated. These teachers had possibly spoken ill of Paul's character and accused him of deceit. Paul, therefore, attempted to exonerate himself. This he did by putting in place a transparent process and procedure for the gathering and delivery of the monetary gifts to the poor Christians in Jerusalem. Paul saw unfaithfulness as inappropriate for believers and knew that it was of utmost importance that a leader is found reliable. No wonder he said: "it is required in stewardship that one be found faithful" (1 Corinthians 4:2).

Secondly, Paul did not only seek to nullify fake accusation, he was ready to act on their accusation as a criticism that needed to be transparently addressed. Paul understood that transparency demands public availability of information. He knew that for information to circulate freely and appropriately within an institution, followers must be free to speak their mind, and leaders must welcome such openness. To address the circulating criticism therefore, Paul included three people of high repute among the emissary for the delivery of the money. This was a careful approach initiated by Paul. He initiated this move to eradicate any suspicion about misappropriation of the fund. His motive was to avoid any iota of criticism or accusation of how the money was handled. Paul understood that to uphold transparency there must be clarity of roles and responsibilities, as well as adequate control which prevents misappropriation or embezzlement. Thus, a brother, chosen by the Churches, was included in the delivery emissary, with the responsibility to "travel with us with this gift". Paul understood that those who administer God's money cannot afford to be secretive with it. If openness is lacking in the Church how can Church leaders admonish the public or those who administer the nation's money to be transparent in their financial stewardship? Paul recognized that the Church is a light unto the world. Thus, the Church is expected to be a leading example to the world especially when it comes to transparent stewardship.

Thirdly, Paul cared greatly about what people thought of his action. He was especially conscious of money issues when dealing with his converts. He had an eagerness to take care of the poor (Galatians 2:10) and knew that to do this on a higher scale, he needed the assistance of other Christians. In order to get others' commitment to the project, they needed to be confident that his action was not to his own profit but for the betterment of the lives of other Christians. In this case: the poor congregants in the Jerusalem Church. Thus, Paul saw transparency as a necessary tool in securing the confidence of the donors.

Fourthly, Paul realized that a Christian ministry that lacks transparency is just another religious organization limited by its leadership intelligence, and not by the unlimited power of God. It thus becomes clear why he was eager to have a member of the Church in Achaia, chosen by the congregation themselves, accompany his team to Jerusalem and witness how they used the money which had been donated by the Achaia congregation. This way, suspicion and side talk would, to a greater extent, be eliminated, thus making Paul and his companions more respected in the entire region of Achaia and beyond. This is an act which aligns with Onora O'Neill's statement: "Transparency is widely supposed to make institutions and their office-holders both more trustworthy and more trusted".[2] Paul understood the need for leaders to demonstrate honesty and integrity by supplying followers with all ministerial information, including them in decision makings, especially those decisions that affect them, and never exploiting or manipulating them.

Lastly, Paul lived his word. He had earlier stated that a conscience that is alien to any hidden agenda is what he and his partners in the ministry possess. He writes: "by manifestation of the truth, commending ourselves to every man's conscience in the sight of God" (2 Corinthians 4:2). To substantiate this therefore, he needed to demonstrate that he had nothing to cover up. As such, his ministerial activities, especially monetary activities must be opened to the scrutiny of the congregants. Paul was conscious of the fact that if his integrity became doubtful among his converts then his ministry could be negatively affected. Hence, he must be above suspicion not only in the Lord's sight but particularly also in the eyes of his converts. Knowing this, Paul deliberately distanced himself from

---

[2] Hood, Christopher. Heald, David. Ed. *TRANSPARENCY The key to better Governance?* New York: Oxford University Press, 2006, 75.

direct contact with the money by not getting involved during the gathering stage, and also by including local delegates among the delivery emissary. This he did to protect his reputation.

When it comes to transparency, the Church is one of the institutions that struggle the most. Church leaders' defense is usually that their actions are between them and God, and that all their actions and in-actions are opened to God. Paul makes it clear that vertical as well as horizontal openness is required in the ministry when he says: "providing honorable things, not only in the sight of the Lord, but also in the sight of men". In other words, actions that are opened to God should also be made visible to mankind.

Financial Transparency: Current Demeanor

Financial obscurity is a major problem in most African nations. The Churches are well positioned by the Apostles to show the world what it meant to be transparent financially. How can this be achieved if a large percentage of Church goers, as well as registered Church members have no clue as regards the finances of their local Church?

Congregants know little or nothing about their Churches finances. No financial information is recorded in any of the bulletins, articles or Sunday service handouts. None of these documents contained any budgetary information or information concerning the amount realized or expensed within the previous week(s) or month(s). Many African Church leaders do not make enough financial information available to their members.

While the local Church leaders have detailed

information about finances, the congregants as well as the subordinate leaders do not. The few subordinate leaders who have some of this information are those directly involved with the Churches' finances like the accountants, or some key members of the Churches' boards or spouses to the local Church leaders.

Learning from Paul's Principle of Financial Transparency

The common area of concealment in most of our Churches is in their failure to disclose financial details to their congregations: an act that does not conform to the culture of candor established by Apostle Paul.

Paul knew that financial transparency requires conscious effort and commitment of the leaders of the ministries. This explains why he ensured that the gathering process, as well as the gathering itself, was transparent to the entire Church in Achaia (1 Corinthians 16:1–4). He also incorporated remarkable checks and balances in the dispatch process. Nothing in the entire process of collecting and dispensing of the money was unclear to the donating Churches. This transparent act helped to ensure commitment of the congregants who gave bountifully towards the liberality. This makes it clear that when transparency is imbibed, genuine honesty is obvious and communal dedication results. Thus, when leaders are open in their dealings with their congregants the result will not only be a condition of trust, but it will in addition make the followers go the extra miles in contributing their skills, time, money and other valuables to a worthy cause. Voluntary commitments would be achieved without the need for leaders to exert pressure on the group, since by being transparent everyone is carried along.

It was the high esteem that Paul had for Christ Jesus, coupled with the grace of God, that enabled him to be an open person – one who did not resort to what he called fleshly wisdom, or a deceptive front involving shrewdness and scheming (2 Corinthians 4:2). He was a man that put the person and way of Christ on display and admonished other Christians to imitate him.

It is a common thing to find organizations that champion or defend financial secrecy and portray it as necessary in some cases. It is important however, to state that financial transparency in the church as well as in the social-cultural communities is not a choice. It is an indispensable collective principle. The more enlightened your congregants are, the more transparency will be demanded. It thus becomes clear that every Christian ministry, as well as other non-profit organizations, must maintain transparency in their financial dealings so that they can remain relevant to future generations.

It is obvious that Church leaders will gain a higher repute by learning from Paul's principle of financial transparency. This repute will qualify them to effect positive changes within their communities and the nations at large. The onus then is on the Churches' overseers and their subordinate leaders to:

- Put in place a clear disclosure policy and ensure that the policy is adhered to within their organizations. Transparent financial procedures need to be clearly written and widely communicated throughout the hierarchical structure by preaching, teachings, town halls, seminars, and conferences. Education, on a large scale, is vital to make transparency possible in the entire Church bodies.

- Make the congregants aware of their entitlements to sound financial transparency and that they can demand it when it is not at their disposal. Congregants should not be made to feel they are in the dark as regards financial matters. This implies that leadership accountability must be upheld in all local Churches. Leaders, within each local Church, must make it a standard to ensure that all financial records such as budgeting, summarized financial statements, as well as the organizations' balance sheets are properly recorded and reported to the donors as and at when due.

- Ensure that in all the local Churches, provision for accurate records of transactions, cash disbursements, and receipts are in place. This includes the proper recording of all allowances given to ministry leaders as well as payments to ministry staffs. There is the need for adequate mechanism and tools for financial control within all local Churches. Each Church body in each country they operate need to have an internal control department to audit the books and ensure compliance. This is important as it demonstrates that adequate accountability, which is void of financial favoritism and faulty accountability, is in place.

- To have mechanisms, processes, and tools which are rendered useless and not complied with is unacceptable. Therefore, steps needed to prosecute and punish offenders anytime malfeasance is found should be in place and be strictly adhere to. Every Christian ministry must ensure that they produce accurate and correct organizational information.

Finally as a supplementary control mechanism, adequate checks and balances need to be in place in all Churches. Africans in all non-profit Christian institutions and organizations need to demand accountability from their leaders more firmly than ever before, and those leaders need to respond in the affirmative. When checks and balances are not in place, misconduct results. To further strengthen checks and balances, it is crucial that every local Church have provisions for a board of trustee or governing board which will be its ultimate administrative and financial body. The board should be appointed by the members of the Church, and chaired by a reputable member other than the pastor or someone who is not at arm's-length to the pastor. The pastor should be the Spiritual head of the Church while the board of trustee's chairperson or the governing board's chairperson should be the administrative head and financial head.

The aforementioned are necessary if our Churches will remain credible and vital to generations yet unborn. Credibility and validity will be a mirage where financial obscurity is a choice, or where leaders chose to promote a false sense of transparency and accountability. Thus, it becomes necessary that false sense of transparency and accountability be repelled and leaders make all financial information as well as other related important information accessible to the entire stakeholders which include the congregants. Only when this is done can a Church leader be reputable before the political leaders of his nation, and this will privilege such a Christian leader to correct the flaws of the political leaders without any fear of intimidation.

CHAPTER THREE

SPEAKING TRUTH TO THE AUTHORITY

Now when Peter had come to Antioch, I withstood him to his face, because he was to be blamed; for before certain men came from James, he would eat with the Gentiles; but when they came, he withdrew and separated himself, fearing those who were of the circumcision. And the rest of the Jews also played the hypocrite with him, so that even Barnabas was carried away with their hypocrisy. But when I saw that they were not straightforward about the truth of the gospel, I said to Peter before them all, "If you, being a Jew, live in the manner of Gentiles and not as the Jews, why do you compel Gentiles to live as Jews?

Galatians 2:11–14

Speaking truth to the authority is one of Christians' most fundamental obligations. It means to provide information honestly and fearlessly to one's superior(s). It neither waters down the need to honour leaders nor encourages disrespect of leaders. Peter Bouteneff in his answer to the meaning of truth replies: "Truth is the reality underlying appearances. We could simply say that something is true when it conforms to genuine, existing reality."[3] Appearance can sometimes be deceiving, but the real truth underneath every false appearance need be expressed.

Antioch Event

It is important to note that immediately following the crucifixion, resurrection and ascension of Jesus Christ around A.D.30,[4] Apostle Peter became the leader of the Church with the Church's headquarter in Jerusalem.[5] As part of the persecution faced by the Church at that time, Peter was imprisoned by King Herod Agrippa I around A.D.41.[6] After imprisonment and liberation from prison,

---

[3] Bouteneff, Peter C. *Sweeter than Honey. Orthodox thinking on Dogma and Truth.* Crestwood, NY: St. Vladimir's Seminary Press, 2006, 21

[4] Schnabel, Eckhard J. *Early Christian Mission. Jesus and the Twelve.* Volume One. Downers Grove, IL: InterVasity Press, 2004, 42.

[5] Dunn, James D. G. *Beginning from Jerusalem. Christianity in the making.* Vol. 2. Grand Rapids, MI: William B. Eerdmans Publishing Company, 2009, 208.

[6] Schnabel, Eckhard J. *Early Christian Mission. Jesus and the Twelve.* Volume One. Downers Grove, IL: InterVasity Press, 2004, 44.

he left Jerusalem (Acts 12:17) and from then on devoted himself to missionary activities. From the time Peter went into the mission field, James, the brother of Jesus took over the leadership of the Church.[7] However, every apostolic and high-levels decisions were usually vested under the joint authority of James, Peter and John (Galatians 2:9).

Not too long before the Jerusalem Council which took place around A.D.49 (Acts 15:1–21); there was a heightened doctrinal crisis on the mission field in A.D.48. Apostle Peter came to Antioch and was eating freely with the Gentiles until some Jewish Christians came from Jerusalem. As soon as they came, Peter withdrew from eating with the Gentile Christians. This presumably was because it was unlawful for a Jew to eat with the Gentiles according to the Jewish tradition:

> While we live in Nineveh, all my relatives and the other Jews used to eat the same kind of food as the other people who lived there, but I refused to do so. Since I took seriously the commands of the Most High God, he made Emperor Shalmaneser respect me, and I was placed in charge of purchasing all the emperor's supplies. (Tobit 1:10b–13, Good News Bible, Old Testament Apocrypha, TEV, Canadian Bible Society)

---

[7] Freeman, Charles. *A new History of Early Christianity*. New Haven, CT: Yale University Press, 2009, 45.

> And do thou, my son Jacob, remember my
> words, and observe the commandments
> of Abraham, thy father: Separate thyself
> from the nations, and eat not with them:
> And do not according to their works,
> and become not their associate; (The
> book of Jubilees 22:16a, Old Testament
> Pseudepigrapha)

Paul did not see the separation of Peter from the Gentiles as a normal Christian way of life. He, therefore, had to correct Peter in the presence of everyone.

The Confrontation

In Antioch, Paul stood up to Peter. The questions are: Why did Paul choose to speak against Peter's withdrawal from the table? Why did he choose to confront Peter publicly?

Truth was Paul's way of life. He was someone who found it uncomfortable to withhold truth (Acts 20:27; Romans 9:1). Peter Bouteneff, in his description of truth as it concerns Christians, opines that it is "linked to a way of life, one that is in concert with the way things really are. Truth is not just something that we learn, it is something we do, how we live. Truth can be an action, an activity."[8] People who live by the truth always find it hard to seal their lips when lies manifest. For Paul, truth was the way he lived and it was his nature to "speak the truth

---

[8] Bouteneff, Peter C. *Sweeter than Honey. Orthodox thinking on Dogma and Truth.* Crestwood, NY: St. Vladimir's Seminary Press, 2006, 22.

in Christ" (1 Timothy 2:7). This explains why he could not hold back his view during the Antioch incident, for he noticed that Peter was "not straightforward about the truth of the gospel" (Galatians 2:14).

In addition to the above, Paul needed to uphold the Christian values of truth and oneness. Paul was convinced that the followers of Christ are expected not to hide the facts but to reveal them even if they do not align well with a leader's preferred course of action (Romans 1:18; 2 Corinthians 13:8). He understood that adding obedience to the law as a requirement for salvation would void the sufficiency of Christ's redemptive work for those who believe. Thus, the onus was on Paul not to indulge Peter, a pillar of the Church, but to equip him with necessary information needed to make the right decision, and for him to always do the right things even if that made Peter uncomfortable.

Also, Paul's intention was to stop the spread of lies. The apostles were the foundation and backbone of the Church (Ephesians 2:20), and congregants tended to follow their examples. Peter's action deceived many Jewish Christians, even Barnabas. It demonstrated an act that seemed to compel the Gentiles to Judaism diet law and religious observance. If Paul failed to correct him, the infiltrating lies at that time which opined that Christians must obey the Jewish law for them to be righteous will spread like wildfire, because Paul's silence would imply approval of Peter's action. Thus, Paul had a duty to speak up for the truth in the presence of all, because, keeping quiet when we ought to speak is tantamount to lying.

Moreover, Paul saw Peter's act as hypocrisy. Paul, as

well as many others, regarded Peter as an authority in the Church. An authority as defined by Friedrich "is an expert, and one so qualify may give his opinion in court".[9] Thus, Paul was convinced that Peter knew the truth about the Gospel (Galatians 2:8) and for him to act contrary to that truth may have negative effect on other believers. Therefore, it became necessary for Paul to confront Peter in the presence of all, so that the Jews present as well as the Gentile congregants can desist from falsehood. Paul detested hypocrisy. His point was: if it was still wrong for Jews to eat with the Gentiles after Christ has died and risen, why did Peter eat with them earlier? If it was not wrong anymore, why did he desist from eating with them later?

Additionally, Paul spoke up to avoid making his calling: a call to the Gentiles – void. Paul had a duty to protect the Gospel which he preached among the Gentiles, though it could have been uncomfortable for him to have confronted a pillar of the Church. However, he saw speaking truth to an authority as a precept that went a long way to defining the value of the speaker. Truth speaking classifies the speaker as either one who contributes positively to his community and the well-being of the people being served or someone who for lack of courage or as a result of temporary reward fails to speak the truth, and let down both Christ and the people being served. Paul knew that people who drew back from speaking truth to authority gradually sold their consciences and eventually played along. He knew that if he failed to speak the truth concerning the issue of the law,

---

[9] Friedrich, Carl J. *Authority*. Cambridge, Massachusetts: The American Society of Political and Legal Philosophy, 1958, 63.

then his calling to the Gentiles would be at risk. Paul was concerned that he needed to demonstrate a behavior that is in total agreement with the Torah-independent gospel he preached. According to the gospel, Christ freed both the Jews and non-Jews from the demands of the law.

Lastly, Paul was following the footstep of his master, Jesus Christ. Just as Paul spoke the truth to Peter, Jesus of Nazareth continually spoke truth to the religious authority of his time. Jesus presented the true interpretation of the law as established on love for God and one-another (Mathew 5:31–32, 15:1–9, 22:34–40; Luke 5:29–32), while Paul went further to establish that the same Jesus is "the end of the law for righteousness to those who believe" (Romans 10:4). Craig A. Loscalzo, in his book *Evangelistic Preaching that Connects*, puts it this way:

> The religious establishment in Jesus time could not tolerate blatant opposition to their authority. In fact, the word was quickly spreading that Jesus taught as one who had authority, not like the scribes. If you want to create a problem with the religious establishment, just get people to start calling into question the way of looking at things. The good news that Jesus and his disciples preached not only didn't make sense to the leadership, it made them mad.[10]

---

[10] Loscalzo, Craig A. *Evangelistic Preaching that Connects. Guidance in shaping Fresh & Apealing Sermons.* Downers Grove, IL: InterVarsity Press, 1995, 45.

The Outcome

The confrontation between Paul and Peter at Antioch could have been the climax of the lingering doctrinal, ethnic, and cultural issues persisting among the Jewish and Gentile Christians for years in the first-century A.D. This issue could have led to the Jerusalem Council which took place around 49 A.D. (Galatians 2:4).

We do not know how many people among Paul's emissary went to Jerusalem for the meeting, but Paul makes it obvious that Barnabas went with him, and they took Titus with them. Titus was an uncircumcised Gentile. Probably Paul wanted to practically display Christian virtues present among Christian Gentiles through Titus. Titus was a Gentile who was strong in love, dedicated to the ministry, and an epitome of faith in Christ Jesus (2 Corinthians 8:6, 8:16, 8:23). To affirm the decision of the Church at the council, Paul writes: "But neither Titus, who was with me, being a Greek, was compelled to be circumcised" (Galatians 2:3).

A major point discussed during this meeting was whether the Jewish laws required by the Torah should be imposed on the Christians. At this meeting, Paul defended the Torah-independent gospel he preached and surprisingly Peter reasoned with Paul and gave instances where he had seen the power of God demonstrated among the Gentiles without their law observance. Possibly, Peter had pondered on the issue leading to the confrontation at Antioch for a reasonable amount of time and had come to the conclusion that law observant is no more a requirement for righteousness. Peter probably realized that he acted wrongly at Antioch by not standing for the truth. With Peter's supporting evidences of the Torah-independent gospel which Paul preached, James was equally convinced that observance of the law was not required to be a Christian. James then gave in with a verdict that the Gentile Christians should not be made to observe the law. He says:

> Therefore I judge that we should not trouble those from the Gentiles who are turning to God, but that we write to them to abstain from sexual immorality, from things strangled, and from blood…..since we have heard that some who went from among us have troubled you with words, unsettling your souls, saying, you must be circumcised and keep the law – to whom we gave no such commandment. It seemed good to us, being assembled with one accord, to send chosen men to you with our beloved Barnabas and Paul, men who have risked their lives for the name of our Lord Jesus Christ. We have therefore sent Judas and Silas, who will also report the same things by word of mouth. (Acts 15:19–20, 24–27).

It thus becomes clear that James, as well as other pillars of the Church, espoused the above position not necessary to satisfy the Gentile Christians, but because they were convicted of the truth and power inherent in the Gospel.

To formalize the Apostles' decision, a letter was written to the Gentile Churches informing them of the decision reached by the pillars of the Church at the Jerusalem Council. In order to authenticate the content of this letter, two brethren from Jerusalem, Barsabas and Silas, were sent to accompany the letter to the Gentile Churches. The two brethren would bear witness along with Barnabas and Paul, on the decision reached by the council concerning the things that are required of the Gentiles in order for them to be part of the Christian body. The decision aimed not to belabour the Gentile converts with the Jewish legalities but to safeguard them from idolatry and sexual immoralities, and to encourage their support for the poor (Acts 15:23-29).

Insights on the Duty to Speak Truth to the Authority

The duty to speak truth to the authority is becoming more relevant in the Church as well as in the society at large. Apostle Paul enjoins Christians to be subject to governing authorities because "there is no authority except from God, and the authorities that exist are appointed by God." (Romans 13:1). These authorities could be such that exist in governments, communities, homes, businesses and Churches. To understand the current demeanor in the Churches of Africa as regards the concept of authority one must gain an insight into how the congregants and the subordinate leaders see and relates with their pastors.

Speaking Truth to Authority:
Current Demeanor

A larger percentage of African pastors believe that they deserve to be treated special by their subordinates and congregants in general. Not all the Church leaders will welcome a correction from their congregants when they are wrong. In like manner:

- Many congregants and subordinate leaders are not disposed to correcting their pastors.
- The smaller the Church the more open the subordinates perceive their pastors to be.

Many of the African Church leaders still have the 'superiority mentality' because of their position as the pastor, reverend, deacon, evangelist, bishop, etc.

How African Christians relate
with their Leaders

Africans pre-Christianity religious beliefs and ideologies play a vital role in the way and manner of approach between the congregants and the leader or between a subordinate leader and the superior leader in the African Churches.

In the pre-Christianity era, the priest consulted the deities on behalf of the people. The priest would inform the people of the deity's messages. In those days, it was a taboo to question, confront or doubt the words of the priest. A priest would not expose the lapses of another priest, even if one of them was not in the right. Their usual saying was that the confraternity is a brotherhood cult that upheld and supported each other under any circumstance. The pre-Christianity Africans regarded the priest as the mouth piece of the deities and anything spoken by the priest was presumed as originating from heaven. As such, it was unacceptable for any member of the community to talk down on or doubt such proclamations.

Similarly, most African Christians see their leaders as above board and someone who should not be questioned, cross-checked or doubted. They see each word that proceeds from their pastors as pronouncements from God. As such, for a congregant to see the truth and speak that truth to the pastor is unacceptable to majority of the congregation. A large number of the pastors also see themselves as above board and superior to their subordinates. The leaders' common quote is: "render honor to whom honor is due" a paraphrase of Romans 13:7. To them, this implies that their congregants are expected to treat them as honorable. Thus, cross-examining or having reservations for words spoken by a Church leader, or a leader's action or in-actions, is usually interpreted as a dishonor.

Pros and Cons of Leader-Followership Style

The leader-followership relationship that is obtainable in African Churches tends to get the job done, for the current generation of African Christians. Money flows in and the mission expands. The mission is however expanding in 1st world nations not because other ethnic or racial groups are being evangelized and converted to Christianity, but because more Africans are migrating into these countries. A substantial amount of the immigrants prefer to worship in a Church that is comparable to those they attended in their home country. This is probably because culture plays an important role in Christian worship.

Through observations and during interviews, it was easy to notice that congregants and subordinate leaders tend to obey their leaders out of fear and/or intimidation, rather than out of love for God's Church and what Christ has done. This type of leader-followership relationship is unhealthy for the local Churches as well as the body of Christ for "God has not given us the spirit of fear, but of love and a sound mind" (2 Timothy 1:7). Service to God and mankind must come from a willing heart for it to be rewarding.

Authority as Revealed by Paul

Authority is a word that is synonymous with "command" – It implies having the ability, by virtue of position, to command subordinates to take certain actions. Authority is a good thing and it is required in any society or gathering of people. Paul gave several usefulness of authority, among which are:

- Authority is meant to be used in building up and not tearing down. Apostle Paul speaks of "our authority, which the Lord gave us for your edification and not for your destruction" (2 Corinthians 10:8, 13:10).
- Authority can be used to order subordinates to do the proper thing. Paul says "though I might be very bold in Christ to command you what is

fitting, yet for love's sake I rather appeal to you" (Philemon 8, 9).

- Authority is to be used in correcting. Titus is charged to exhort and rebuke with all authority (Titus 2:15).
- In addition to authority being used for correction, it can also be used in dispute settling (1 Timothy 5:19–20).
- Christian authority can also be used to cast out demons, set the captives free and deliver the oppressed. Having observed the numerous miracles and healings performed by Jesus, the chief priest and elders challenged him: "By what authority are you doing these things, and who gave you this authority?" (Mathew 21:23; Mark 11:28; Luke 20:2). Jesus also gave his disciples "power and authority" over demons, to cure diseases, and tread upon serpents when he sent them out on a mission (Luke 9:1–2, Luke 10:19).

Improving Leader-Followership Relationship to boost Truth Speaking to Authority

As good as authority is, a major defect is that it can also be an instrument of destruction in the hands of a bad leader. Saint Thomas Aquinas submits in his book *Summa Contra Gentiles* when he opines: "A thing that one can use both for good and for evil cannot be man's highest good."[11] Though authority is needful, it can however be used for evil. It thus becomes imperative for all Christians, most especially the subordinate leaders, to:

- Devote their time to studying. Paul admonishes Timothy, one of his subordinate leaders, to give attention to reading (1 Timothy 4:13). Paul sees reading as one of the tools required by a subordinate leader to gain knowledge of the truth, for his master, Jesus Christ says: "You shall know the truth, and the truth shall make you free" (John 8:32). It is crucial for subordinate leaders not to see themselves as mere cheer leaders for the people in authority. Every subordinate also has a level of authority which needs to be used in support of truth and against all lies.

- Be diligent in their duties. People who are diligent at their work or assignments are void of eye service. They pay attention to details, and consequently become proficient in their gifts. This makes them vital resource to the Church and enhances confidence in the one who has called them. This way, they are apt to speak the truth at all times without fear of being ousted.

- All lieutenants in the Church need to be entrenched in love so as to get rid of their fear. Perfect love, John says "cast out all fear" (1 John 4:8). Some subordinate leaders want to tell the

---

[11] Aquinas, Saint Thomas. *Summa Contra Gentiles. Book Three. Providence Part 1.* Garden City, New York: Hanover House, 1956, 118.

truth but are too scared to do so for fear of being ousted, rebuked or punished. The love for God, for their leaders, and the people served, should empower them to refrain from all lies and to stand by the truth at all times.

It is imperative that all subordinates desist from being senseless collaborators in lies, and wrong doings. All the atrocities committed by leaders whether in government, community, or Church are purely enhanced because majority of those who are their immediate subordinates fail to speak the truth to them. A candid advice is this: every lieutenant should focus on speaking the truth at all times especially to those in authority so as not to make void their callings. Regent Morton when speaking at John Knox's graveside says: "Here lies one who neither flattered nor feared any flesh"[12] . The inability to speak truth to authority is an expensive deficiency which had cost the human race a great fortune. The Nazi extermination of the Jews from 1933 to 1945, the brutal and inhuman reign of Idi Amin of Urganda, numerous ethnic killings in various parts of the world, various perpetuation of African leaders in power, the embezzlement and misappropriation of funds by those in authority, and similar other barbaric leadership practices are examples of what results when lieutenants chose to flatter their leaders and collaborate in lies, rather than speak truth to them. Inhuman policies, which sometimes originate in the mind of a leader, could be avoided from taking roots if lieutenants are apt in

[12] McGreggor, L. G. *The Thundering Scot*. Philadephia, PA: Westminister Press, 1947, 226.

speaking truth to their leaders. It is therefore crucial that every Christian should resist all attempts to promote lies, and be diligent in upholding the truth at all times. The question then is: Are leaders able to absorb the truth when it is spoken to them, whether done constructively or unconstructively, knowing that truth is most times bitter?

Authority's Response to Truth

Paul withstood Peter "to his face" in Antioch (Galatians 2:11), and corrected him over dietary law before the entire Christians present (Galatians 2:14). After this, there was no evidence that Peter tried to justify or rationalize his action, neither did we learn that Peter presented Paul to the rest of the Church "pillars" (Galatians 2:9) for disciplinary action. Rather, many scholars believe that Peter took Paul's correction in good faith. Ian C. Levy posits:

> It was with holiness and kindness that Peter accepted in pious humility what Paul had so usefully achieved through the freedom of charity. Peter thereby provided later generations with an example that it is as saintly as it is difficult to imitate, when one considers the fact that most highly placed officials will not even deign to yield the right of way at crossroads, let alone

> allow themselves to be corrected by their underlings.[13]

It is no news that many Church leaders have positioned themselves as implacable authoritarians: supreme commanders who give orders that no one would dare to question. This is not something learned from the scripture neither is there any such example of a spiritual leader in the Bible. We have seen in the books of the Bible where mortal beings question the plans of God. Abraham questioned Gods plan to destroy Sodom and Gomorrah and even negotiated with the Most High. Before the destruction of Sodom, Lot negotiated with the Lord. He bargained with God's Angels when he thought escaping to Zoar is a better option than running to the mountains. Moses debated with God when asked to go back to Egypt and rescue the Israelites from the hands of Pharaoh. Jonah was more aggressive in his discontentment with God's decision to relent from bringing disaster on the people of Nineveh. So, where then did we learn the human authoritarian supremacy over the flocks of God?

If African Church leaders, as well as other Christian leaders, learn to embrace Peter's humble spirit and become receptive to listening to their subordinates when truth is being offered, it will to a great extent vitalize Christianity and make the rest of the world see Christians as they are expected to be – "the light of the world" (Mathew 5:14).

---

[13] Levy, Ian Christopher. Trans. and ed. *The bible in Medieval Tradition: The letter to the Galatians.* Grand Rapids, MI: William B. Eerdmans Publishing Company, 2011, 194.

Getting Things Done Without the Use of Authority

Since authority can be used for both good and evil, it thus becomes necessary for every leader in the Church not to rely on the use of authority to get things done. Rather, Church leaders, like Paul, need to understand how to get things done without the use of authority. To do this, they must: First, learn the role of trust, credibility, respect, and integrity for getting results. We all have a duty to act with integrity and in good faith. This is because, everyone respect those who have integrity as virtue, though not everyone like them. Second, understand and continually apply the principles that help in building cooperation with co-workers. Third, learn how to overcome the common obstacles to getting results without the use of authority. Fourth, identify and appreciate the indispensable outcomes of leading with accountability and transparency. Fifth, understand those steps that need to be taken in overcoming self-doubt and building self-confidence.

Summarily, since the level of integrity possessed by each individual differs, this makes Paul's admonition to the Roman Christians relevant. He advises: "pursue the things which make for peace and the building up of one another" (Romans 14:19). Speaking truth to the authority is one of the effective ways we build up our leaders and prevent them from errors. Therefore, in order to prevent most blunders within the Christian communities, it becomes a perpetual duty for subordinates within African Churches to always speak the truth to their leaders. This has the tendency to make the Christian race less laborious, and the world a better place.

Similarly, every godly leader must not be indifferent to the suffering of the people in his nation of service. In Archbishop Desmond Tutu's words, "if you are neutral in situations of injustice, you have chosen the side of the oppressor". It thus becomes clear that a genuine leader must do all that is necessary to ease the suffering of the populace, and this includes preaching, teaching, and speaking against corruption at all times. Then, all can join Apostle Paul in saying: "I tell the truth in Christ, I am not lying, my conscience also bearing me witness in the Holy Spirit" (Romans 9:1).

CHAPTER FOUR

FINANCIAL INDEPENDENCE

But we command you, brethren, in the name of our lord Jesus Christ that you withdraw from every brother who walks disorderly and not according to the tradition which he received from us. For you yourselves know how you ought to follow us, for we were not disorderly among you; nor did we eat anyone's bread free of charge, but worked with labour and toil night and day, that we might not be a burden to any of you, not because we do not have authority, but to make ourselves an example of how you should follow us. For even when we were with you, we commanded you this: If anyone will not work, neither shall he eat. For we hear that there are some who walk among you in a disorderly manner, not working at all, but are busybodies. Now those who are such we command and exhort through our Lord Jesus Christ that they work in quietness and eat their own bread. But as for you, brethren, do not grow weary in doing good. And if anyone does not obey our word in this epistle, note that person and do not keep company with him, that he may be ashamed. Yet do not count him as an enemy, but admonish him as a brother.

2 Thessalonians 3:6–12

The Church community in Thessalonica had been plagued with laziness on the part of some of its members: through their refusal to work. Paul termed those involved in this act as "busybodies", and commanded (with the authority of Jesus Christ) those who were working and those who were willing to work that they withdrew support from those who refused to work.

Refusal to work, according to Paul, is an open opposition to the apostolic tradition. Thus Paul instructs not only the leaders but the entire congregation to mark down those in this category. The purpose of the withdrawal, in this case, was to make the persons in question feel ashamed. "And if anyone does not obey our word in this epistle, note that person and do not keep company with him, that he may be ashamed" (2 Thessalonians 3:14) says Paul. It was a punishment meant to produce soberness and an amendment of life, "For godly sorrow produces repentance leading to salvation, not to be regretted, but the sorrow of the world produces death" (2 Corinthians 7:10). Withdrawal from the lazy members will also serve to purge the community of disorderly influences they could have on those who worked or were willing to work.

The injunction against those who refused to work was that they should not be privileged to eat. In other words, only those who work are entitled to eat. Jeremiah was tough while speaking about the relationship between work and wages. He says "Woe to him who …uses his neighbour's service without wages and gives him nothing for his work" (Jeremiah 22:13). Jesus was more subtle, he said "The labourer is worthy of his wages" (Luke 10:7). These speeches invariably mean that those who work deserve their wages, and those who do not work deserve no wage. Paul therefore admonishes that those who work should withdraw the generous act of giving from those who refuse to work. They should not be allowed to benefit from benevolent offering of the congregation either. That way, they are prevented from profiting out of the labour of the industrious ones. Paul's command, "if anyone will not work, neither shall he eat", is a way of discouraging idleness among Christians. The apostle provided the Thessalonians with justification for withdrawing support to those who preferred to rely on the generosity of others rather than work themselves.

Paul was a working minister. He worked as a tent maker during the day and sometimes at night. In reference to his accompanists: "we labouring night and day" is his word. Consequently, he sees those who refuse to work as "working disorderly" and not following after his footsteps.

When self-sufficiency is the subject, Paul and his co-missionaries were protagonists to the Christians.

It seems perhaps Paul viewed these "busybodies" as exploiters since some converts were doing good work in faith by diligently going about their businesses and being generous, but others saw these good gestures and were exploiting them by being idle. Paul needed to warn the good congregants against resignation so that those who were unable to work among them would not be negatively affected by his command.

Personal feeling of hostility towards the persons in question was not what Paul wanted but for them to be shunned, and no alms extended to them. This was to make them ashamed and subsequently repent from their disorderly conduct. Thus, the attitude Paul expected from those who had refrained from deliberately being idle in the community was not a superior, loveless one but that which disciplined in love.

Paul understood that instigating hate and enmity in a community contradicts the basic principle of Christianity which is "to love one another". Thus, he says despite all punishments against the 'busybodies', the working believers should remember that they must still remain brethren to those working disorderly because human emotions and hate can lead to unfitting actions.

Jesus gave room for those who preach the gospel to eat of the gospel (Luke 9:4, 10:3–7). This is a directive in line with Moses' guideline that those who serve at the altar are privileged to eat of the altar. Paul knew that he and his colleagues had the right to refrain from working (1 Corinthians 9:6–14; 1 Timothy 5:18), but chose not to take advantage of the situation. Why? Why did Paul choose to work while ministering in Thessalonica and some other places?

It appears that Paul and at least Barnabas also, are exceptional among the apostles by not exercising their right to cease from working. This principle prevented them from becoming dependent on the generosity of their converts. Paul's reasons for choosing to work while in ministry could include some of the points highlighted below.

Firstly, though Paul and his company had the right to refrain from working, they did not exercise this right because Paul loved his converts so dearly: "We were well pleased to impart to you not only the gospel of God, but also our own lives, because you had become dear to us" (1 Thessalonians 2:8). No wonder he gave up the right to eat of the gospel (Luke 10:7; 1 Corinthians 9:6) by working just as his converts did. This is because love voluntarily gives up those things which it could lay claim to and raises a selfless objection against all self-centeredness and injustice. This makes the words of Ben Witherington III clearer: "Paul will follow the deliberative rhetorical strategy of appealing to the need for equity as honourable behaviour: all should work if they wish to eat"[14].

Secondly, Paul chose not to work because he was a loving leader. His desire was not to be a burden on his converts. Rather, his major concern was to model a culture of financial independence among those who preached the Gospel and have this replicated to those they taught

---

[14] Witherington, Ben III. *1 and 2 Thessalonians. A socio-rhetorical commentary.* Grand Rapids, MI: William B. Eardmanns, 2006, 247.

also. Paul's decision to work while in ministry was a clear demonstration of true fatherly adoption of his converts. Just as a good father will not want to be a burden on his children, so was Paul determined not to be a burden on those he has adopted as children through the gospel. As a father therefore, Paul intended to teach his converts to be financially independent. He saw idleness as inappropriate for believers and thus he needed to establish a culture of financial independence through his example – "but to make ourselves an example of how you should follow us".

Thirdly, Paul did not want to depend on the goodwill of others for his livelihood. He wanted to be able to support himself financially. He constantly reminded his converts of how diligently he and his companions worked: "that we might not be a burden to any of you". He wanted not just to support himself, but also to support others (Acts 20:34–35) especially the weak. It was his choice not to be a burden on his hosts (Acts 18:1–3). Working while ministering enabled him to support his hosts, most times, with grocery expenses, Paul says: "nor did we eat anyone's bread free of charge" (2 Thessalonians 3:8).

Fourthly, Paul needed to make obvious the fact that he did not distort the word of God because of his needs (2 Corinthians 4:2) neither did he exploit his converts by taking advantage of them or manipulating them (2 Corinthians 11:20). To be able to do this, and declare the whole council of God (Acts 20:27) without fear of intimidation, he needed to have a means of sustaining himself apart from the generosity of those he taught. This way he could avoid improper payments and distinguish himself from those he termed as disreputable teachers with whom he never wanted his converts to associate (1 Corinthians 9:12; 1 Thessalonians 1:5, 2:3–6; Acts 20:33–35). Doing this, Paul intentionally kept a virtuous testimony. By working for his needs with his own hands he avoided any appearance of financial motives. He provided his converts especially the Thessalonians and Corinthians with concrete evidence that his motives in preaching the gospel were not duplicitous.

Fifthly, Paul wanted to distinguish himself from the many disreputable teachers who made a living peddling the message of salvation (2 Corinthians 2:17) He was concerned that for his message to remain credible there should be no element of self-interest in it. Ben Witherington III comments: "One reason Paul may have been sensitive about this point and why he set such an example of work is that philosophers were notorious for being busybodies and also for living off of patrons, whom they served as tutors or rhetors"[15]

Lastly, Paul took this energetic step to prevent false ideas from taking root as the norms within the Christian community. Presumably, some had begun to see Christianity as a cover for laziness since they could peddle the gospel and rely on the generous acts of their listeners for their livelihood. This is an easier means of livelihood than having to work in a secular field. Paul wanted to demonstrate that propagating the gospel does not, would not, and perhaps cannot hinder one from working in the secular field or running a business on the side.

In summary, Paul did all these so as not to hinder the

---

[15] Witherington, Ben III. *1 and 2 Thessalonians. A socio-rhetorical commentary.* Grand Rapids, MI: William B. Eardmanns, 2006, 253.

spread of the Gospel in any way. He was single-minded on the proclamation of the Gospel, and would not toy with anything which could prevent its acceptance. The choice to work while in the ministry was not without its hardships, but Paul was willing to endure the hardships because of the burning desire within him. His mind was progressively saturated with the gospel, and with the unequalled excellence and supremacy of the Lordship of the risen Christ. He was, therefore, willing to do all that was necessary for the Gentiles to see the truth of the Gospel he brought to them. For the sake of the gospel therefore, Paul laboured night and day. The labour "night and day" mentioned in Paul's letter was a way of summarizing the suffering he endured. The suffering that Paul had imposed upon himself simply to support himself for the sake of the gospel.

Paul sometimes accepted financial support as revealed in his Letter to the Philippians (Philippians 4:15–19). This happened mostly when he was continually moving from one location to another or during the periods he was in prison. This was simply because he could not work at those periods. At other times, he clearly rejected financial support, conspicuously in Corinth (1 Corinthians 9). However, his general ministry principle was to maintain financial independence. He mentioned that he worked to support himself in many of the New Testament literatures (Acts 20:34; 1 Thessalonians 2:9; 2 Thessalonians 3:8; 1 Corinthians 4:12, 9:6; 2 Corinthians 12:13–14).

Financial Independence: Common Practice

The common practice these days is that most people who minister in the things of God want to be financially compensated. Many of the people who teach or play an instrument in the Church are on the payroll with the pastors not exempted. Some Christian denominations encourage financial independence by searching for volunteers in all spheres of the ministry within the Church. This is usually effective in situations where the group's leader is also engaged in secular job or entrepreneurship and does not depend on the Church funds for his/her upkeep.

Exploring Paul's Principle of Financial Independence

The New Testament literature is in support of Church leader being supported from the Church's fund while at the same time encouraging Church leaders to be financially productive. One of the impediments to the advancement of the gospel is the financial dependence of brethren on the Churches' purses. Many of the leaders in our Churches do not have a means of livelihood apart from the Church. This can be improved when leaders start and do some legitimate business on the side. I was privileged to meet a pastor whose congregant was about 700 people at that time. This pastor runs a real estate business on the side. Helps people to buy and sell properties. For him, he does not do it to get compensated as a realtor, but allows those he helps to freely compensate him as they desire after the deal is completed. Another financially independent pastor I met in Africa oversees over one thousand members. He runs an average-sized piggery farm and informed me that he makes substantial amount yearly from this business.

Paul refers to "not working" as a disorderly conduct.

This is a behavior that goes contrary to the tradition of financial independence he established among the Christians. Here are some of his statements:

> And we labor, working with our own hands. Being reviled, we bless; being persecuted, we endure. 1 Corinthians 4:12.

> For you remember, brethren, our labor and travail; for laboring night and day, that we might not be a burden to any of you, we preached to you the gospel of God. 1 Thessalonians 2:9.

"Be thou followers of me" (1 Corinthians 4:16, 11:1) is Paul's statement. He also gave a protagonist's statement in Philippians 3:17, when he said "Brethren, join in following my example, and note those who so walk, as you have us for a pattern" (Philippians 3:17). While Paul's convert could agree with his pure motives and upright conduct, they also saw in him a repute leader that is worthy of emulation. When we discuss the issue of financial independence in the ministry, Paul is an ideal model. The question then is: How can the African Churches benefit from Paul's principle of financial independence?

Firstly, not working can be infectious in the Church. Ministry leaders' unwillingness to work while in the ministry kills the missions since this infects the communities like a plague. Every Christian, whether a new believer, or someone who is developing, or the advanced leader of a group is admonished by Paul to apply his ability to be resourceful and not depend on support from other brethren. By working, each Christian is able to take care of his household's needs and also give to the weak, for "it is more blessing to give than to receive" (Acts 20:35) says Paul. It thus proves that when the practice of financial independence is championed by the fore-leader, it circulates down the hierarchy, and the entire church body becomes rid of economic dependants.

Secondly, when Church leaders work, it reduces the burden on the congregants and increases the fund available for other ministry essentials. Here is what William Corey wrote about working while on Christian mission: "We have ever had it to be an essential principle in the conduct of missions, that whenever it is practicable, missionaries should support themselves in whole or in part through their own exertions."[16] Followers learn from their leaders. Thus, when leaders work, the followers also learn to work.

Thirdly, work is a boost to self-respect, self-discovery, and self-confidence. Above all, there is dignity in labor. Paul boasted many times about his working-ministry practices. Working while in ministry increases the self-worth of the leader before his congregants, especially where a large amount of the congregants are learned and belong in the working class. Just like Paul, a working leader, is then qualified to admonish his congregants on the need to work and not be a burden on others or the nation's welfare fund. This, if morally examined, has altogether to do with what is proper behavior for the followers of Christ. To further reduce the burden on the Churches, voluntary services need to be encouraged and

---

[16] Grubb, Kenneth Sir. *The Need for Non-professional Missionaries.* London, England: World Dominion Press, 1931, 11.

the ball must start with the leadership. A working leader is able to elaborate on his example as a guide for voluntary services since the leader is also doing the work of God without charge. Action, it is said, speaks louder than voice. The leader is able to teach in this regard by example, and all are able to emulate him.

Fourthly, Paul was not egocentric. He knew a great deal about selflessness. He was a person who willingly gave time, money and life for Christ. Working as a tent-maker meant earning little income and living below average. This certainly would not have provided the apostle with much income to be able to give to others, but he still managed to give from the little he earned. He was particularly concerned about the poor saints of Judea, and did all he could to procure funds for them (Acts 11:29–30, 24:17; Romans 15:25–27; 1 Corinthians 16:1; 2 Corinthians 8:9). Paul taught the Christians what it meant to be contented. He taught the Christians the art of being alien to self-centeredness. By working while doing the work of God, leaders teach their followers the art of 'Godliness with contentment'.

Fifth, flexibility is a requirement in the ministry, and leaders can be more flexible if they are willing to do what it takes to remain free to do and say and go wherever Christ calls them. This explains Paul's methodology of using his tent-making abilities to remain independent so he could be flexible with his approach to the ministry. There are huge advantages to a great work ethic. A Church leader who is tied to the income received from his Church may visibly not be in the position to fully speak and teach the truth to his congregants or subordinates since they pay his salary. A leader who earns his pay from other legal sources, and not dependent fully on the Church is able to speak the truth in love when it is required.

Summarily, Apostle Paul's resources played an important role in his walk with Christ. He had few material assets, but bountiful spiritual assets which he used in his call to the Gentiles. One major catalyst to Paul's labor while in the ministry was the love he had for his converts. Love for one's neighbor is centered on justice – "do unto others as you wish to be done unto" (Mathew 7:12; Luke 6:31). People who do not like to work but prefer to depend on other believers' generous giving for support, offend against justice. All Church leaders must therefore strife not to be a burden on their Church's purse. Everyone has the right and duty to eat from the bread that he has earned himself and be a donor to every contribution within the Christian community. Anytime the local Church contributes towards an event or project, a leader should neither exempt self nor be exempted. Rather, leaders should show leadership example by being the first to cheerfully contribute "for God loves a cheerful giver" (2 Corinthians 9:7).

In certain circumstances, it may be fair for the Church leader to be on the payroll and compensated in proportion to his rating by the Church governing body. However, many Churches in the so called developing nations are founded and run by a single person. This makes it difficult for the governing council of the Church (if there is any) to take any decision which does not align with the wish of the leader. Such decision automatically becomes void since the founder or CEO as the case may be will overrule it. However, an ideal situation for a Church leader who cannot work because of the huge ministerial responsibilities or conditions will be for him to be on the payroll and be content with his pay and allowances as determined by the Church's governing body.

As leaders, our thoughts should be on how to increase available funds for ministry essentials. Thus, each one of us need to be engaged with the questions: In God's service, how can I make myself independent of the funds that come into the ministry's purse? Am I able to develop a trade, a business or skill which can help reduce my dependence on the Church fund? What can I do to help reduce staff's pay or totally eliminate salaries from the expense list of the ministry? People who have no financial attachment to an organization's fund are able to address issues and speak impartially. They can more readily welcome transfer to other branches of the Church, even if the congregants in the new Church are fewer and the Church remotely located.

CHAPTER FIVE

TEACHING THROUGH PRACTICE

A ministry leader who intends to change life must live what he teaches. In the case of Paul, he taught more by who he became and what he did after his encounter with Christ Jesus. Paul was an example of a teacher who taught more by action rather than words. That is why he was able to say "imitate me as I imitate Christ" (1 Corinthians 11:1). Paul's day-to-day life demonstrated that whoever must teach need to be an exemplary character because the most important measure of a teacher is how genuine he himself is. The followings are few of the many ways in which Paul taught practically:

Sacrificial Service

Apostle Paul lived what he taught. He could teach about love because he was a loving leader; he could teach about giving because he was always willing to give all he had and all he was: "I will very gladly spend and be spent for your souls; though the more abundantly I love you, the less I am loved" (2 Corinthians 12:15). In the Acts of Paul and Thelca 23 we see a practical way Paul unintentionally taught self-denial, faithful stewardship, lovely and selfless giving:

> And Paul was fasting with Onesiphorus and his wife, and his children, in a new tomb, on the way which led from Iconium to Daphine. And when many days were past in fasting, the children said to Paul: "We are hungry." And they had nothing to buy bread, for Onesiphorus had left the things of this world, and followed Paul, with his house. And Paul, having taken off his cloak, said, "Go, my child, sell this and buy some loaves and bring them." And when the child was buying he saw Thelca their neighbour, and was astonished and said, "Thelca, whither art thou going?" And she said, "I have been saved from the fire, and am following Paul." And the child said, "Come, I shall take thee to him, for he is distressed about thee and prays and is fasting already six days".[17]

Onesiphorus (also mentioned in 2 Timothy 1:16–18) and his household were family friends to Paul. Paul had probably taught his friends and converts the secret of

---

[17] Pick, Bernhard. *The Apocryphal Acts of Paul, Peter, John, Andrew and Thomas.* Chicago, IL: The Open Court Publishing Company, 1909, 23.

spiritual warfare through fasting and prayer, and they had joined him in his petition to God for Thelca who most likely had been arrested by the Roman government. Here, Paul offered his cloak in return for food for their sustenance. Paul had the habit of giving and sacrificing for his converts: "For the children ought not to lay up for the parents, but the parents for the children" (2 Corinthians 12:14). Paul says he does not seek what the converts have, but they themselves. He continually sought their souls for Christ and laboured to see them grow and develop into matured Christians. He taught the love of Christ by his life, through his conducts, and devotion. He was an example of someone who gave it all. This explains why he cautioned the Christians to think more of the treasure they carry, the message they proclaim, the heaven to which they are invited than the material gains, the finances or the popularity gained (Philippians 3:17–21).

Paul cared for those he shepherded and was constantly investing personally in their lives (Acts 20:31). He was a caring and encouraging father to his converts (1 Corinthians 4:14–17; 1 Thessalonians 2:7–11). The love of Christ was a major influence in Paul's ministry, and it was Christ's love that compelled him to live his life out for Christ. In his letter to the Corinthians he declares: "For the love of Christ compels us, because we judge thus: that if One died for all, then all died; and He died for all, that those who live should live no longer for themselves, but for Him who died for them and rose again" (2 Corinthians 5:14–15). Christ's love made Paul to serve sacrificially and devotedly.

Paul understood the details of the ministry he received from the Lord Jesus (Acts 20:24), and had a single eye towards finishing his course with joy. This explains why he had no need for any material accumulation, for he believed in the grandeur of the heavens than the human structures of this earth (1 Corinthians 15:19; Philippians 1:23; Titus 2:13).

Paul had unshaken confidence in the person of Christ Jesus. He believed and taught that God's love for the Christians was secured in and through Jesus. Nothing, says Paul, is able to put asunder the relationship between God and a Christian because of what Christ Jesus had done (Romans 8:38–39). No wonder he laid all his attainments at the foot of the cross and gave himself fully to Christ. In his Letter to the Philippians (Philippians 2:17–30) he uses the metaphor of a drink offering to illustrate his sacrificial service on behalf of Christ. In the Old Testament, the priests do offer two animal sacrifices daily. These animals were usually spread on the altar to be consumed by fire. As part of the daily offering, there was a drink offering of wine which was poured out to the Lord (Exodus 29:38–41; Numbers 28:7). Paul considered it an honour to be poured out to the one he saw as Lord, and have his life totally used up in the service of Christ. No wonder he admonishes believers to give themselves to God as living sacrifices (Romans 12:2). The questions then are: As a minister of the Gospel, am I able to give sacrificially to those under me without expecting anything back? Is my giving focussed on those who have no means of paying back or I do give with the mindset of an investor? Is my ministry truly supporting the poor and the vulnerable among the congregants? Do I see and feel the pains of those who are less privileged in my community, state and nation, or am I focussed on the things of this life which passes away?

Adaptability in the life of Paul

> For though I am free from all men, I have
> made myself a servant to all, that I might
> win the more; and to the Jews I became as
> a Jew, that I might win Jews; to those who
> are under the law, as under the law, that
> I might win those who are under the law;
> to those who are without law, as without
> law (not being without law toward God,
> but under law toward Christ), that I
> might win those who are without law; to
> the weak I became as weak, that I might
> win the weak. I have become all things
> to all men that I might by all means save
> some. Now this I do for the gospel's sake,
> that I may be partaker of it with you. 1
> Corinthians 9:19–23

To the Jews, Paul was a Jew. To the Gentiles, he was a Gentile. To the Romans, he was a Roman citizen. He was many things to many people. This adaptability in many ways propelled his ministerial success. Paul's behaviour of becoming all things to all people is not a strategy aimed to please people (Galatians 1:10) and thus make the gospel somehow less powerful (Romans 1:16). Rather, it is a way of teaching that all members of the Church must be willing to adapt their behaviours for the sake of the gospel (Philippians 1:27).

Paul laid down his high status as a Pharisee and associated with the poor and the rich, the educated as well as the unschooled. He was ever ready to see himself in other people's shoes, experience their pains and endured their struggles in order to position himself well enough for the propagation of the gospel. His association with all levels of mankind was mainly to win some of them to Christ.

In the first-century AD Roman citizenship was a key measure of status and significance. Therefore, Paul's status as an educated Roman citizen would indicate that the apostle had enjoyed some elite social standing prior to his Damascus road encounter with Christ, and that he had truly demeaned himself by taking up tent making as a profession in order to offer the gospel free of charge. No wonder he was confident to say of himself as "not marketing God's word for profit" (2 Corinthians 2:17). His motives were geared toward gaining more souls to Christ. This he did by always looking for those who were most receptive to the Gospel (Acts 18:6).

In general, people are reluctant to make adjustments to changing situations, but Paul knew how to make the necessary changes to enhance the success of his ministry. For example, immediately following his encounter with Christ he spent some days with the disciples at Damascus (Acts 9:19). He was able to make necessary changes from his earlier status as an educated elite to living as a tent maker. No doubt his choice of taking up manual job must have knocked him down the social cadre. He, however, did it voluntarily and joyfully for the excellence of Christ Jesus whom he acknowledged as Lord and Saviour. His evangelism approach in Athens was public while it tended towards private evangelism in Corinth. He constantly adjusted his agenda to accommodate the needs of his audience without compromising his principles. To the Philippians he affirms: "I know how to be abased, and I know how to abound. Everywhere and in all things I have learned both to be full and to be hungry, both to abound and to suffer need." (Philippians 4:12). Paul presented himself as one who willingly restricts his own freedom for the benefit of others. To do this, discipline, flexibility, as well as self-control is needed.

Paul kept his message and ministry simple. He did this by focusing on Christ's priorities of evangelism and discipleship (Acts 14:21). He was always willing and ready to adapt to changes. All his ministerial as well as extra-ministerial activities were geared towards promoting a purposeful Christian life which relied on the power of Christ (Philippians 4:13).

Total Dedication to Ministry

> Are they Hebrews? So am I. Are they Israelites? So am I. Are they the seed of Abraham? So am I. Are they ministers of Christ?—I speak as a fool—I am more: in labours more abundant, in stripes above measure, in prisons more frequently, in deaths often. From the Jews five times I received forty stripes minus one. Three times I was beaten with rods; once I was stoned; three times I was shipwrecked; a night and a day I have been in the deep;

> in journeys often, in perils of waters, in
> perils of robbers, in perils of my own
> countrymen, in perils of the Gentiles, in
> perils in the city, in perils in the wilderness,
> in perils in the sea, in perils among
> false brethren; in weariness and toil, in
> sleeplessness often, in hunger and thirst,
> in fasting often, in cold and nakedness—
> besides the other things, what comes
> upon me daily: my deep concern for all
> the Churches. Who is weak, and I am not
> weak? Who is made to stumble, and I do
> not burn with indignation? 2 Corinthians
> 11:22–29.

Paul was qualified to teach his subordinates about dedication to their callings because no other person can be compared to him in ability, energy, passion and dedication devoted in the mission to the Gentiles. Paul's words were always confirmed by his life. His subordinates, converts, and followers always saw him as a picture of his own words.

Paul's calling as a minister of Christ is most important to him. Thus, his suffering on behalf of Jesus Christ was of secondary consideration in as much as Christ is preached. His imprisonments, shipwrecks, weariness, hunger, perils, beatings, and close encounters with death were of little or no issue to him as long as Christ's kingdom kept expanding. For Paul, the apostolic ministry is a continual and progressive sacrifice for the excellence of Christ.

The magnitude of sufferings Paul endured for the sake

of the Gospel was incredible. He however responded to them positively and took them as part of his commitment to Christ. He also viewed them as necessary instruments to the attainment of eternal glory (2 Corinthians 4:17). In his sufferings, hardships and persecutions he hung on to the greatest gifts – faith, hope and love, and strongly believed in the ever present help of Christ in all the trials he encountered (Acts 23:11, 27:23; 2 Timothy 4:17).

Paul was a distinguished ministry leader. A coach who displayed all distinguishing leadership qualities, such as: focus, motive, mission and enviable moral standard. He was totally dedicated to the calling he received and worked hard at converting his followers into disciples who were able to carry on the mission after him (2 Timothy 1:6, 4:2, 2:24).

Paul was a learner. He was a devoted student of the Scriptures. Very prayerful and had a systematic habit of devotion and scripture study (2 Timothy 4:13; Acts 16:21–22, 27:21–25; Romans 9:1–4) which explains why he could present the Christian life as a privilege and not a burden.

Paul never saw ministry leadership as a ladder to something else in this life. He served Christ wholeheartedly in accordance to Christ's leading. His mission to the Gentiles was in line with the calling he received from Christ Jesus (Acts 9:1–30, 21:33–22:21, 26:1–29). The daily burden upon him was a deep concern for the body of Christ than for himself. Scott J. Hafemann synchronizes it thus:

> Paul's statement in 2 Cor. 11:7a that he humbled himself in order that the

> Corinthians might be exalted also recalls
> Paul's prior principles in 2 Cor. 10:24 that
> one should not seek his own good, but the
> good of his or her neighbour.[18]

It was Paul's "deep concern for all the Churches" which gave him the spiritual energy, power, and unequalled persistence to live the life that he did. He was truly dedicated to the extent that he could say: for him to live was Christ; that the life he lived in the flesh, his thoughts and actions were all the result of Christ living in him and through him.

Paul was constantly targeting new groups (Romans 11:1), penetrating new territories (Romans 15:20), and inventing new strategies (Acts 13:14, 44–49) to reach his potential converts. In the face of cruel and unfair treatment, Paul maintained a thankful attitude (Acts 16:25) and never backed down or gave up.

Therefore, these are the questions one should ask oneself: As a leader, am I dedicated to the ministry I have received? Do I see ministry leadership as a ladder to wealth, fame or power? Ability to correctly answer these questions will to a large extent determine how positively we can impact our generation and those yet unborn. Therefore, a Christian leader should not be among those who defend and/or aid looters of treasury, whose greed and insatiable love for money and power has devastated the continents of Africa and mortgaged the future of her youths. A Christian leader should not be seen to collect from those

---

[18] Hafemann, Scott J. *Suffering & Ministry in the Spirit.* Grand Rapids, MI: William B. Eerdmans Publishing Company, 1990, 151.

whose lifestyles do not equate their income. Those whose voraciousness have kept the nations down as third world countries. If only we can spare a moment and think it through, just as others before us had died and never went with a penny, so shall each one of us one day in the future go without a cent. Apostle Paul standardized this in his words to Timothy "For we brought nothing into this world, and it is certain we can carry nothing out" (1 Timothy 6:7). When Christian leaders are totally dedicated to their call, then they are able to admonish others, especially the nation's leaders to be dedicated to the office they occupy and the people they are meant to serve.

A Disciplined Life

> Do you not know that those who run in a race all run, but one receives the prize? Run in such a way that you may obtain it. And everyone who competes for the prize is temperate in all things. Now they do it to obtain a perishable crown, but we for an imperishable crown. Therefore I run thus: not with uncertainty. Thus I fight: not as one who beats the air. But I discipline my body and bring it into subjection, lest, when I have preached to others, I myself should become disqualified. 1 Corinthians 9:24–27.

Self-discipline in Paul's ministry cannot be overemphasized. "But I disciplined my body" is his statement. To Paul, discipline is a self-conscious characteristic which requires a deliberate effort. So, he made a great effort to subdue his fleshly desires "and bring it into subjection", thus making room for the desires of his Spirit man. Instead of being a follower of his bodily appetites, he exercised self-restraint and made every effort to lead them. This way, his entire body served his gospel mission.

Paul equates the Christian life to a race in which the participants aim at obtaining a prize. In order to obtain this prize of imperishable crown, Paul makes it clear that being "temperate in all things" (1 Corinthians 9:25) is a requirement. No wonder in his letter to the Philippians he admonishes them to "let your moderation be known unto all men" (Philippians 4:5a, KJV). Self-discipline, self-control, moderation, and the likes are required virtues for effective Christian service. Exercising these qualities on a consistent basis, build up the Christian's spiritual stamina. A Christian is then concretized with endurance, strength, balance and flexibility needed for an effective Christian life. Knowing this, Paul, therefore, made it a requirement to discipline himself.

Paul disciplined not only his body, but his mind also. In his Letter to the Corinthians he explicitly states that the weapons used by Christians for warfare are such that bring "every thought into captivity to the obedience of Christ" (2 Corinthians 10:5). Paul thus advises that disciplining the mind helps the Christians to effectively use the divine weapons needed to cripple all demonic powers and thoughts, and make them submissive to the lordship of Christ. Thus, Paul comported himself by disciplining his mind along with his body. Why did Paul choose to discipline himself?

One, Paul made it clear that he would not want to "become disqualified". In other words, he aimed at receiving a prize for his Christian labour. He did not want to suffer loss (1 Corinthians 3:14–15). It thus was required of him to put in place measures that will guarantee his obtaining the prize. The first paramount measure, therefore, is self-discipline. According to success expert Napoleon Hill, self-discipline is:

> One of the Twelve Riches, but it is much more; it is an important prerequisite for the attainment of all riches, including freedom of body and mind, power and fame, and all the material things that we call wealth. It is the sole means by which one may focus the mind upon the objective of a Definite Major Purpose.[19]

Paul had a major purpose after his encounter with the risen Jesus: to preach Christ and his crucifixion. It thus becomes apparent that the passion, zeal, courage, and perseverance he displayed in the ministry can partially be a product of his self-discipline which was geared towards this definite major purpose. Napoleon posits that those who do not exercise self-discipline "suffer the loss of a great

---

[19] Hill, Napoleon. *The Master-Key to Riches*. New York, NY: Penguin Group Inc., 2007, 242.

power which they need in their struggle for achievement of their definite chief aim."[20]

Two, Paul understood the importance of self-discipline in working with God. He did not advocate an indiscipline personality. He was convinced that the Christian personnel should be well disciplined both in mind and in body.

He beseeched the Christians in Rome to be "transformed by the renewing of your mind" (Romans 12:2). He admonished the Philippians to keep their minds occupied with whatever was true, noble, just, pure, lovely, of good report, and praiseworthy (Philippians 4:8). He exhorted Timothy to exercise spiritual discipline and devote himself to it (1Timothy 4:7–8). He reasoned with kings and rulers on the issue of righteousness, the judgement to come and self-control (Acts 24:25). He warned Christians about the danger associated with the lack of self-control (1 Corinthians 7:5, 7:9; 2 Timothy 3:3). In his Letter to the Galatians he included self-control as a fruit of the Spirit (Galatians 5:22–24). Peter supports Paul's view when he states:

> But also for this very reason, giving all diligence, add to your faith virtue, to virtue knowledge, to knowledge self-control, to self-control perseverance, to perseverance godliness, to godliness brotherly kindness, and to brotherly kindness love (2 Peter 1:5–7).

---

[20] Hill, Napoleon. *The Law of Success. Complete and Unabridged.* Blacksburg, VA: Wilder Publications Inc., 2011, 270.

Paul says without holiness no one can see God. This can simply be because Paul understands that self-discipline is a requirement for moral thrust, which cannot be ignored by the person that wants to work in holiness. The moral impetus implied here is not limited to sexual immorality, bribery and lies alone. It is such that conducts itself in uprightness and does not call evil, good. A man's word should be his bond. Isaiah makes this clear in his writing:

> Woe to those who call evil good, and good evil; Who put darkness for light, and light for darkness; Who put bitter for sweet, and sweet for bitter! Woe to those who are wise in their own eyes, And prudent in their own sight! Woe to men mighty at drinking wine, Woe to men valiant for mixing intoxicating drink, Who justify the wicked for a bribe, And take away justice from the righteous man! Isaiah 5:20–23.

Three, Paul knew that to teach and lead others, one must first teach and lead himself. He thus chose to be a role model to his converts. He was not drawn back from promoting self-discipline in his numerous letters because he practiced it and people could see it in him. Andrew Carnegie writes: "the man who acquires the ability to take full possession of his own mind may take possession of everything else to which he is justly entitled."[21]

Paul understood that self-discipline is a compelling attribute expected of a leader. It makes or breaks a leader, and provides people with a compelling reason to either follow or not. Thus, it is important for him as someone with a singular mission of preaching Christ, to dedicate himself fully to self-discipline.

As a leader, how disciplined are you? A leader needs to be disciplined when others are watching as well as when no one is watching, knowing that nothing is obscure "to Him, whom we must give account" (Hebrew 4:13). Only a disciplined leader will have the courage and audacity to call to order the political leaders in his nation. The singular reason why some of our spiritual leaders cannot speak against the malfunctions of the political leaders is simply because their records are not clean. They have secrets which are open to the politicians and these can be used against them if they chose to speak truth when required. Some who do not have skeleton in their cupboard have at one time in the past cut corners. They have requested inappropriate favors from the political leaders and this has shut their mouth up forever. Where a Christian leader is not disciplined, then there will be skeletons in his cupboard. Skeletons in the cupboard of any religious leader will hamper him from speaking against the ills in his nation. The truth is: If our nations must survive, those who champion the course of Christianity must be above board when discipline is considered. Our Christian leaders

---

[21] Hill, Napoleon. *The Master-Key to Riches.* New York, NY: Penguin Group Inc., 2007, 240.

need be able to tell the Herods of our time that corrupt practices are wrong and unlawful. We need Christian leaders to rise up and be the leading voice among those whom the political leaders will fear and respect based on the knowledge that they are just and upright, and will not represent darkness as light (Mark 6:20).

Learning from Paul's Practical Approach to Teaching

The first step to excellence in the ministry is dedication. Apostle Paul sacrificed all that he had and all that he was for the Gospel. This demonstrates to mankind that those who accept the call to the Christian ministry must be ready to sacrifice self and serve others. All Christian leaders and especially those in the African Churches need to follow the footsteps of those who laid the foundation of this noble faith through their selfless services. There must be a determination for dedication to duty. Christian leaders must desist from seeing ministry leadership as a tool for financial accomplishment. Leadership in Christianity must not be handled as hirelings, but as a good shepherd (John 10:12–13). This way, ministry accomplishments are not counted in dollars and cents but in the number of souls that come to the knowledge of Christ and develop into His nature.

Though Christian leaders are encouraged to work and earn some income in order to be unbiased leaders like Paul, the ministry must be every Christian leader's primary commitment. A Christian leader must be zealously consumed with regard to the conversion of men, as an immediate business. Christian leaders must be willing to endure all things for the sake of those under them. Paul says he "endured all things for the sake of the elect" (2 Timothy 2:10).

The concept of servant-leadership, as established by Paul, needs to be imbibed by African leaders. Not the ineffective, redundant servant-leadership as practiced by some African political leaders, but the highest quality servant-leadership, as exemplified by this great apostle. Christian leaders are presumed slaves of Jesus Christ (Romans 1:1, Philippians 1:1, Jude 1:1). This means that they take instructions and directions from Jesus. A Christian leader is not just a slave of Jesus, but also a slave of the community he belongs as portrayed by Paul: "For we do not preach ourselves, but Christ Jesus the Lord, and ourselves your bondservants for Jesus' sake" (2 Corinthians 4:5). Paul made himself slave to all that he might win the more (1 Corinthians 9:19). This way, he taught Christian ministry leaders that they are not to expect to be ministered unto, but to minister (Mark 10:45) unto others. This does not negate the fact that they have the right to physically profit from the congregants. Rather, it means they should not see these rights as conditions for the service they render to the flocks of God. The Apostle Paul admonishes brethren to:

> Recognize those who labor among them
> and are over them in the Lord, and esteem
> them very highly in love for their work's
> sake (1 Thessalonians 5:12–13).

> If we have sown unto you spiritual things,
> is it a great thing if we shall reap your
> canal things? (1 Corinthians 9:11).

Therefore, while the congregants are to be encouraged to physically and financially give unto their leaders, leaders are not to depend solely on the congregants' benevolence.

To conclude this chapter and as a means of striking it all down in reality, I will take a not too serious but none the less honest look at this issue which is killing the African nations before the very eyes of the whole world. A defect in not imitating Apostle Paul's comport principle may not necessarily result in the decline of Churches numeric growth in the short run. It will result in a weak Church. It could mean having a Church that is numerically strong but biblically weak. It could mean a Church whose congregants are highly religious but Godless. It could result in a Church which is physically a body of Christ with no attachment to the spirit of Christ.

Paul set a high standard of integrity, consistency, and honesty with his life. By his life, he set an example for ministry leaders to follow. His conduct aligned with what he taught (1 Corinthians 4:17). Paul never pretended to be what he was not. He never down played his weaknesses. Rather, he admitted his inadequacies, fears, and trembling (Romans 7:15–20; 1 Corinthians 2:3; 2 Corinthians 13:4). He was a man who made known the greatness of God through his dependence on Christ's power (2 Corinthians 12:9). It thus becomes imperative for African Christian leaders to uphold and align with Paul's comport principles in order to have an effective Church. This would be a

Church that will not only meet the needs of this generation and that of the next, but also stand out in her divine mission to the world.

A church that sits on the fence is detestable to God. So, Church leaders must not be indifference to the sufferings of the people. The Church of the Laodiceans was self-righteous and self-sufficient. She was neither cold nor hot. Meaning she was indifferent. Christ says he will spew her out of his mouth. Jesus was not indifferent to the suffering of the people. While he did not cast away the rich, he was constantly taking care of the poor and needy. He constantly spoke against the oppressions and impositions of the Pharisees and the Sadducees. In our days however, most Church leaders have become self-contained, and materialistic, to the extent that they care less about the welfare of the people they lead. We need to consciously keep in mind that our love for Christ is best demonstrated when we show our love for others. This includes those in the Church as well as those outside the Church.

CHAPTER SIX

CONCLUSION

Paul's comport principles examined in this work are practical guides for Christian leaders. Before concluding, something should be said about the practicability of the identified principles established by Paul. There is no doubt that many Church leaders will find it uncomfortable to fully express the comport principles displayed by this servant of Christ. It may also be a gaffe to represent his approach to the ministry as idealistic. While it differs from ministry leaderships' views of our time (and his time) and bypasses the more regimented structured design in which most ministries operate, it does not sprout from an unrealistic model viewpoint. It resulted from a sober reflection of his perception of the risen Jesus and how those who accept him as lord and savior should showcase him.

It will be unfair to discredit the few African Christian leaders who act as voices to the underprivileged by denouncing corruption at every opportunity they have. These handful ministers of the Gospel are already on the right path. They speak loud and clear against Corruption. They act for justice, and against corrupt practises.

Without mixing words however, it is objectively clear that most Christian leaders in the African continent have failed and fallen short of not only the glory of God, but also of the expectations of the righteous. We have sacrificed the future of Africa on the altar of greed and succeeded in producing Christians who are near to God with their mouths, but whose hearts are far from Him. God says: "In vain they worship me" (Mathew 15:9). Corruption in the form of abuse of power is a recurrent problem everywhere in the African continent. Our public sector as well as the private counterpart suffers because offices are abused. Our value system is corrupt and the Christian establishments are aiding and promoting this corrupt value system by their teachings, practices, utterances on the pulpit, and approaches to day-to-day events. The word of Prophet Micah is true today for Africa as it was for the Israelites during the eight-century B.C. when he says: "Her heads judge for a bribe, her priests teach for pay, and her prophets divine for money. Yet they lean on the Lord, and say, "Is not the Lord among us? No harm can come upon us." (Micah 3:11). Is it not true that our priests teach for pay? And our prophets divine for money? The time has come for Christian leaders who are mouth piece of God to teach and speak against bribery, stealing, embezzlement, greed, fund misappropriation, injustice, laziness and abuse of power. This we need to do not only by words of mouth, but majorly by our examples. We are to lead by examples while continually speaking for justice, integrity, hard work, innovations, moderation, contentment, self-control, honesty and faith that are complemented with good works. Not the deceitful propagation of the concept that success will come through prayers, faith and religious offerings. This concept has so far helped to promote religion that is void of Godliness. It has heightened corruption; relegated hard work and belittled ethical moral behaviours by incubating Christians without conscience when genuine love for others comes in question.

Beyond any shadow of doubt, the distinguishing mark of Apostle Paul and his numerous teams was their approach, passion, idealism, dedication and devotion to the cause. These attributes, coupled with integrity to truth, and willingness to sacrifice all, characterized Paul wherever he went. Paul was completely convinced of the fact that Christ is all in all. Thus, he was careful in all that he did, making mention that all Christians one day will meet with his master and Lord of all, Jesus Christ, on the judgment seat. In anticipation of this meeting, Paul took time to ensure that all he did in the ministry were to the service of his master and not for personal gain. He was an epitome of a purposeful life. A comport life that accounted for his great variety of attitude towards Jesus and the gospel. These are embodiments of principles which evidenced the supremacy of Jesus Christ whom he served wholeheartedly, and this should be the desire of every Christian leader. Our conducts and teachings should be such that denounce corrupt practices in all facets. Doing this bequeaths our followers with good examples to follow and Africans will gradually stop celebrating corrupt people, but rather get them stigmatized. This will be a practice with potential to systematically advance our value system because of its ability to renew our minds. The change will not only bring out the best in us as followers of Christ, it will also make our nations great.

ABOUT THE AUTHOR

The author is a co-founder of Sanctified Word Ministry. He had been a member of a foremost African Originated Church in Canada for 11 years. During this period, he was a Sunday School Teacher for over 8 years and the Director of Programs for over 6 years. He was also a member of the Church's Board of Trustees for more than 5 years. His role as the Director of Programs gave him ample opportunity to interact with the leadership of the Church body and that of the other African Originated Churches within Canada and the United States.

The author works as an Information Technology Professional, with a leading global Information Technology Organization. He has a Doctor of Philosophy degree in Apologetics and Theology from Trinity College and Seminary. Currently, he conducts seminars and workshops in a variety of ecumenical settings.

Printed in the United States
By Bookmasters